Facts About the Giant Anteater

By Lisa Strattin

© 2016 Lisa Strattin

Revised 2022 © Lisa Strattin

FREE BOOK

FREE FOR ALL SUBSCRIBERS

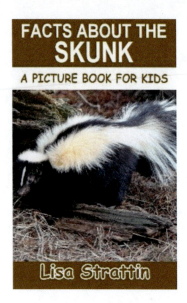

LisaStrattin.com/Subscribe-Here

BOX SET

- FACTS ABOUT THE POISON DART FROGS
- FACTS ABOUT THE THREE TOED SLOTH
- FACTS ABOUT THE RED PANDA
- FACTS ABOUT THE SEAHORSE
- FACTS ABOUT THE PLATYPUS
- FACTS ABOUT THE REINDEER
- FACTS ABOUT THE PANTHER
- FACTS ABOUT THE SIBERIAN HUSKY

LisaStrattin.com/BookBundle

Facts for Kids Picture Books by Lisa Strattin

Sign Up for New Release Emails Here

LisaStrattin.com/subscribe-here

COVER IMAGE

https://www.flickr.com/photos/dionhinchcliffe/12222312336/

ADDITIONAL IMAGES

https://www.flickr.com/photos/37467370@N08/7633428678/

https://www.flickr.com/photos/wagner-machado-carlos-lemes/49164285811/

https://www.flickr.com/photos/cuatrok77/9606738857/

https://www.flickr.com/photos/ekilby/39098728155/

https://www.flickr.com/photos/cuatrok77/9610020366/

https://www.flickr.com/photos/ekilby/27990367148/

https://www.flickr.com/photos/ekilby/27990365748/

https://www.flickr.com/photos/cuatrok77/9606798617/

https://www.flickr.com/photos/cuatrok77/10946203636/

https://www.flickr.com/photos/cuatrok77/10946405616/

Contents

INTRODUCTION

The Giant Anteater is one of those animals whose characteristics are distinct from other animals. Usually when we analyze the food habits of any living creature we think of their size, but this animal-dependent on eating ants is bigger than many other animals. That's why, in some areas, it is called the *Ant Bear*.

The Giant Anteater is one of the largest insect-eating animals living on the earth.

The Giant Anteater, whose scientific name is *Myrmecophaga tridactyla,* has characteristics that are similar to sloths. This is why they are in the Pilosa order of animals. While sloths prefer to live on the trees because ants can be found easily there, the Giant Anteater lives on the ground.

This animal has very long claws and the tail is branchy and bushy. In order to dig the ground, so it can reach the ants, it has a long and hard snout. Its fur is a grayish color.

CHARACTERISTICS

The Giant Anteater lives on the ground whether it lives in the rainforest or grassland, because there are plenty of ants in both of these environments. They are found anywhere in Central America and most of South America due to the rich grasses and forests.

They eat mostly ants and termites by digging into the ground to get to them. The animal uses its strong claws and sucks them up with its extremely long snout and grabs them with a very sticky tongue.

HABITAT

Though the Giant Anteater is found mainly in forests of Central and South Americas, it can also be found in some parts of North America. They are also seen in Honduras. Fossil researchers have found evidence of them being in the western Sonora of Mexico as well, even though they don't seem to be living in this area any more.

There are future possibilities of extinction of these large animals in places like Belize, Costa Rica, and Guatemala. People have played a part in the destruction of habitats for the Giant Anteaters. They have been hunted for leather goods, as well as their paws and teeth.

The Giant Anteater is considered endangered. Since they thrive on the ants that live in trees, losing forests to fires has placed the anteaters at great risk of low food supply.

So, between humans hunting them and the natural forest fires, the Anteater has a lot to overcome in order to remain on Earth!

APPEARANCE AND SIZE

The Giant Anteater has a very large, long, and extruded muzzle, which is very bushy. It also has a long tail and greyish black appearance.

The total body length of the Giant Anteater varies from almost 6 feet long to just over 7 feet long. The average male weighs from 72 to 90 pounds and average female weighs from 59 to 85 pounds.

The snout of the Giant Anteater is said to be the longest animal snout of any animal on earth! The head, all by itself, has an average length of 12 inches.

They cannot see very well. But their noses are very sensitive, which helps them to find food! Many researchers say that it is about 40 times more sensitive than the human nose.

LIFE SPAN

The Giant Anteater's life span is around 16 years.

DIET

The ants and the termites are its favorite food. These are easily available in the grassy ground. This is why you can find the Giant Anteater during the day eating them up. They have no teeth and cannot move their jaw like other animals. Their lower jaw is divided into two parts. They move those two parts to eat. Their saliva is very thick and sticky which helps them to get these small bugs!

FRIENDS

The Giant Anteater lives in a group around a specific home area. But even though they live in a group, they are very solitary animals.

They search for and find food alone. They are aggressive only when looking for and choosing a mating partner to create a family.

The Giant Anteater feeds its babies till the weaning period and the mama carries them around on her back when they are young.

SUITABILITY AS PETS

The Giant Anteater is a wild animal. Due to the specific characteristics like eating habits and behavior with mates, it is impossible to keep the Giant Anteater as a pet.

They need to be able to go into the wild and hunt for their own food. If you want to see them, you should check out your local zoo to see if they have some in an appropriate habitat.

COLOR ME

COLOR ME

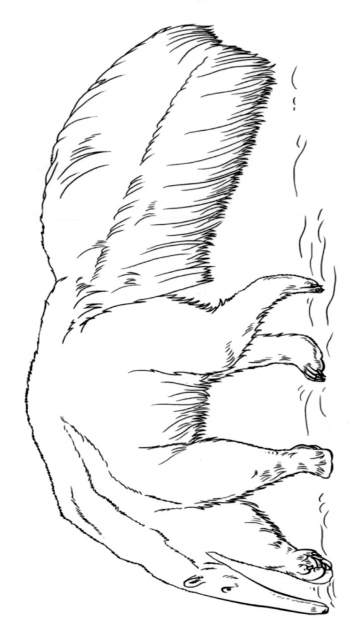

COLOR ME

COLOR ME

COLOR ME

COLOR ME

COLOR ME

COLOR ME

COLOR ME

COLOR ME

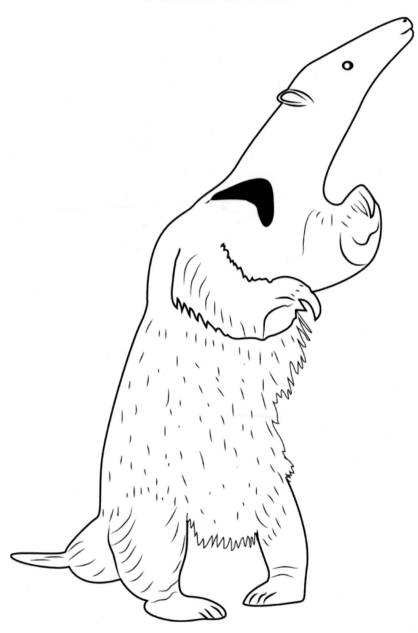

Please leave me a review here:

LisaStrattin.com/Review-Vol-56

For more Kindle Downloads Visit Lisa Strattin Author Page on Amazon Author Central

amazon.com/author/lisastrattin

To see upcoming titles, visit my website at LisaStrattin.com– most books available on Kindle!

LisaStrattin.com

FREE BOOK

FOR ALL SUBSCRIBERS – SIGN UP NOW

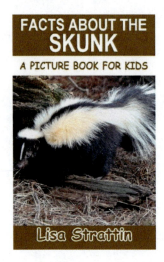

LisaStrattin.com/Subscribe-Here

LisaStrattin.com/Facebook

LisaStrattin.com/Youtube

Made in the USA
Coppell, TX
13 December 2024